I Wish I Lived- WHEN JESUS DID

by
Geoffrey T. Bull
Illustrated by Chris Higham

Pickering & Inglis
LONDON — GLASGOW

Printed in Great Britain
ISBN 0 7208 2245-9
Cat. No. 11/3502

I sometimes wish a wish you know
Then all at once away I go
Across the fields and o'er the trees,
Back through the years, just as I please,
Until I light upon some place,
Or see, maybe, a kindly face;
And then I ask myself, 'Who's that?'
And start to wonder where I'm at.
It's fun to ring the changes so,
To let my mind run to and fro,
For I can be both here and there,
When curled up tight in Mummy's chair.

But, you'd never guess, one day
Where I landed far away.
What a crowd of folk I found;
Shouting, talking, laughter, sound;
Brothers twelve, a sister too,
Husbands, wives and babies, who
Played around amidst the pens
With the goats and sheep and hens.
What a farmyard, topsy-turvy!
Why, it almost made me nervy!

'Joseph!' Jacob called his son,
Next to Ben the youngest one.
'Come!' he said, 'and go for me.
Find out where your brothers be.
Tell me how they feed the flock.'
Joseph went; but what a shock!

When he found them things
    were bad.
Father Jacob would be sad.
Yet he could not hide their sin.
Thus his brothers hated him.

Jacob thought young Joseph loyal,
Gave to him a garment royal.
It was such a fine
new coat
But his brothers soon
took note,
Saying with a jealous fuss,
'Father loves him more
than us!'

Not long after Joseph dreamed.
Oh, how strange the story seemed!
All the family cutting corn,
Binding sheaves one sunny morn.
Setting stooks up, one by one;
Then to Joseph's, all bowed down.

Soon he dreamed a dream once more,
Rather like he dreamed before.
This time though, he saw the sky,
The sun and moon and stars on high.
Then suddenly they moved around
Young Joseph, standing on the ground.

He told them everything he'd seen.
They wondered what such dreams
might mean.
   Then Father Jacob sternly said
'How can our family bow
   the head
To you, of all my sons,
   the son
    Who, but for Ben
    is the youngest one?

His brothers listened, faces grim.
And all the more they hated him.

And then one day they got their chance;
A rather special circumstance.
The brothers, watching sheep afar
Could see young Joseph coming near.
'Here's the boy who has the dreams!
Let us think of cunning schemes
That will rid us of our brother,
Who has caused us all this bother.'

So they made their cruel attack;
Tore the coat from off his back.
Threw him down a dreadful hole,
Dark as night and black as coal.
Joseph hardly dared to think;
There was not a drop to drink.

As to God his plight he tells,
Hark! The sound of tinkling bells;
Grunts of camels, human voices,
Such a lot of funny noises.
All at once he's lifted out,
Wondering what it's all about.
'Here's the slave!' one brother cries,
'Twenty pieces! That's the price!'
'It's a deal!' the strangers say;
Then they lead the boy away.

Down to Egypt Joseph goes;
Lost to home and those he loves.
There he serves in someone's house,
Till the mistress starts to grouse;
Till by lies she has him placed
In a prison cell, disgraced.

There men put his feet in chains;
Soon he's full of aches and pains.
But again, he's very good
And by all, it's understood,
God is with him in the cell;
And He loves him very well.
So the butler of the King
With the baker, wondering,
What their dreams might
    also hold,
Seek his help and they
    are told.

For the baker there's no hope.
'Hang him!' said the King, 'with rope.'
But the butler, lifted up,
Once again fills Pharoah's cup.
'Don't forget me,' Joseph says;
Thus he waits and still he prays.
Yet that butler in the court,
Gives to Joseph, not one thought,
Till King Pharoah, late one night
Has two dreams and gets a fright.

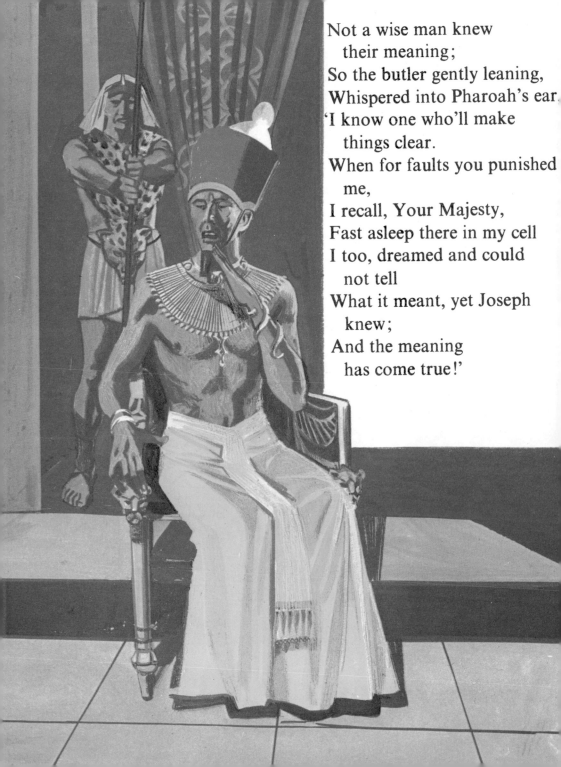

Not a wise man knew
  their meaning;
So the butler gently leaning,
Whispered into Pharoah's ear
'I know one who'll make
  things clear.
When for faults you punished
  me,
I recall, Your Majesty,
Fast asleep there in my cell
I too, dreamed and could
  not tell
What it meant, yet Joseph
  knew;
And the meaning
  has come true!'

'Fetch him quickly!' Pharoah said.
'Give him clothes and with all speed
Set him free and bring him here!
Then we'll see who'll make things clear.'
So he told his dreams with care
And Joseph listened, standing there.

'At first I saw seven big fat cows,
Beside the river quietly browse,
But seven others weak and thin
Came up and seemed to swallow them.
Then seven ears of wheat grew up,
It looked to me, a splendid crop.
But seven ears, all poor and lean
Came in where those first seven had been.'
Thus Pharoah spoke and told his story;
But to God belonged the glory,
For young Joseph, on Him leaning,
Through His Spirit, told the meaning.

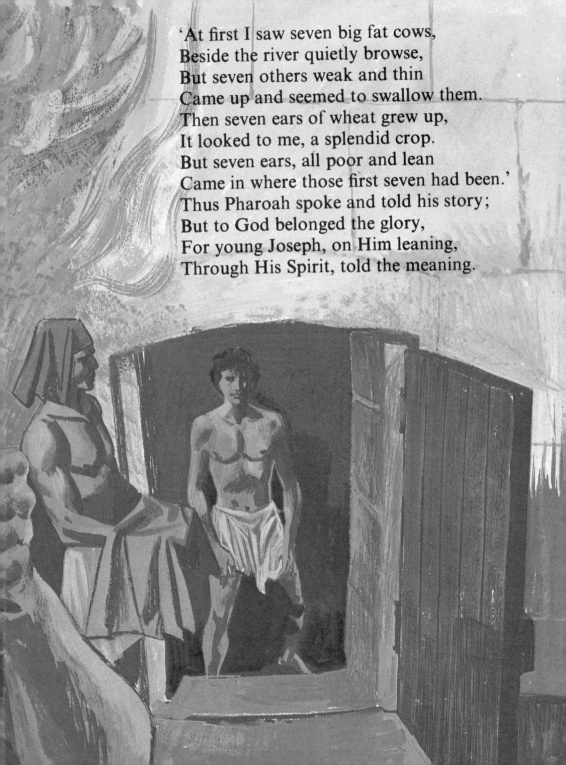

'Seven years of plenty,' Joseph said,
'Will be as nothing for your bread,
When seven years of famine follow
And your hopes of wealth prove hollow.
Make you barns; store all you may;
Then share it out in famine's day.'
Said Pharoah, 'God has spoken here.
You shall be my Prime Minister!'

So, when in time the famine came,
And Jacob heard of Egypt's bread,
He sent ten sons, and in God's Name,
He prayed they all might yet be fed.
They knew not Joseph at first sight.
He called them spies. Oh, what a fright!
He asked of Jacob; tested them.
He wanted to see Benjamin.
So one of them he kept till they
Should bring his brother
    Ben some day.

They came and went, then came again,
And when at last the truth was known,
They bowed before him for the grain
And all the mercy he had shown.
What they had meant for evil then,
God now had over-ruled for good.
'You've saved our lives, we truly own.'
And Joseph quietly thanked his God.